Hates

God ~~Loves~~ You Just the Way You Are

We have this as a sure and steadfast anchor of the soul, a hope that enters into the inner place behind the curtain, where Jesus has gone as a forerunner on our behalf, having become a high priest forever after the order of Melchizedek. (Hebrews 6:19-20)

(Cover photo: 18th Century anchor in Bantry, Ireland)

Hates

God ~~Loves~~ You Just the Way You Are

Michael A. Thompson

God Hates You Just the Way You Are

Copyright © 2011 by Michael A. Thompson

ISBN-10: 061546646X
ISBN-13: 978-0615466460

Published by Charis Publications,
P.O.Box 5116, Kingwood, Texas 77325.

Dedication

To all the Systematic Theology students at Northeast Christian Academy in Kingwood, Texas. May their understanding of and love for the true God of the Scriptures rule their lives, and may they continue the pursuit of truth wherever it may lead.

Acknowledgement

To my wife, Cindy, for her unending love,
suggestions, and encouragement, and for her
passionate example in living out the
instructions given to a godly wife in
1 Peter 3:1-2.

To the inspiration of a saint long past from
this earth, George Whitefield (1714-1770),
who knew the gospel of God as well as any
man and preached it without apology
and unequaled eloquence for more than
thirty-five years, right up until
the day of his death.

To the Reader

This book is written to and for Christians. If the reader is not a Christian, the language, thinking, and emphasis throughout will be relationally unintelligible.

This is a book that is written because of a concern for the truth. The further the church departs from the truth of God's word, as revealed in the pages of the Bible, the further the power and witness of the church is degraded. Ours is a desperate time. Now, more than ever, our own culture and that of others need the spiritual and moral leadership that the Christian church alone can provide. And yet, the church of our time is, for the most part, unable and unwilling to step up to its responsibilities.

The source of the problem can only be one of two things, either: (1) biblical illiteracy, or (2) unbelief. In the Christian church today we are woefully ignorant of the Bible—God's inerrant word. We have access to it as no age ever has had before, yet we are more ignorant of it than at any time since the completion of the canon in the first century.

And as big as the problem of biblical illiteracy is, the second problem, unbelief, is a bigger, more serious one. The unbelief I mean comes in two varieties. First, this unbelief could be an unbelief that the Bible is the inspired word of God. Or second, unbelief in God Himself. Either variety is debilitating—either one is deadly for the church.

But what else could be the cause of the state of the church today? For such aimless waywardness to grip and control our churches, it must be either that we have given up on the Bible as the all-sufficient guide for faith and practice for the Christian; or, we do not believe that God exists at all.

We are in big trouble. And the trouble does not come from the recent rise of militant atheism, the growth of antagonistic governments, or any other external cause. The issue is an internal one. It is an issue of the heart, and an issue of the mind. Part of the problem begs the question: Are our churches being led by pastors dedicated to shepherding God's flock with the spiritual compass of the gospel of the Lord Jesus

Christ? Or are they false guides, seeking security and a paycheck, instead of the spiritual welfare of the flock for which they have charge?

The other part of the crisis, this issue of the heart, comes not from the church's leaders, but from the various congregations themselves. Because we are so intent about dragging just about anyone we can find into our churches, our congregations are comprised of primarily unregenerate people—people who have not been born again and have no relationship with Jesus Christ. No wonder there is no interest in the Bible or even God Himself!

The result is the blind leading the blind—and weak churches worshipping without purpose or direction, ignorant of the church's history, its doctrine, and its responsibilities.

It is because of a love for the church and a deep concern for the truth that I have written the following. The Lord's will be done.

M. Thompson

Prologue

Picture this. It is Friday night at 8:30 at the local mega-church, and the youth group is meeting in a separate annex building of the church "campus complex." Emblazoned across the front outside wall of the annex building are five-foot high letters spray-painted in black and red that say, "Extreme." Inside the building are over 200 kids aged 13 through 17 who are standing and clapping, having just finished singing the third of three popular rock-Christian hits lead by the "Extreme" band. The designated adult-in-charge is the "senior youth pastor," aided by his two assistant youth pastors, and three teen-aged "interns."

Now that the music is over and everyone is seated, the youth pastor takes over the microphone and begins the "lesson" for the evening. The core of his lesson, which he is convinced is based on the teachings of the Bible, goes something like this:

> Life as a teenager in the 21st century is complex and difficult. And the choices you make will define what sort of life you will lead, and whether or not you will end up being a credit or a disgrace to the Lord. But take heart. God has not left you to handle all of life by yourself. God is your great friend. He will help you through all that you will have to face. Always remember, people, that God loves you. He loves you just the way you are. Even with the sin that you are struggling with and all the things you have done wrong, God will never leave you or forsake you. And even though you might be wondering what life is all about, never forget that God loves you and me and accepts us just the way we are.

The youth pastor then read a single verse of Scripture, John 16:27, to convince his hearers of the truth he had stated. One fifteen year-old girl began to sob quietly, admitting to her friend that she was so "happy" that God loved her, especially after what she had done last week. The "Extreme" band then played another two songs, a short prayer was lead by one of the interns, and the group adjourned to the back of the room for refreshments before heading home at 10:00.

Chapter 1:
The Problem

There is a dreadful and deceptive problem in the words of the youth pastor in our little scenario. But before any issue can be dealt with properly and accurately, the problem itself must be fully and precisely identified and defined.

- So what is the problem? So what's the problem with what the youth pastor said? Where is the offense? Life *is* hard in the 21st century, and our choices *will* affect many things that occur in our lives. And God has not left us to fend for ourselves—at least for those of us who know Him personally and have a relationship with Him. His promise for true Christians is that He will never leave us nor forsake us (Heb.13:5). But the youth pastor's statement to his audience does contain a major theological error, at least if you are a Christian believer. The problem is the pastor's assertion that God "....loves you just the way you are.... God loves you and me and accepts us just the way we are." It is a problem because it is not true. Nowhere in the Scriptures, Old Testament or New Testament, does God accept us just the way we are. The rest of this book will analyze this erroneous statement, its implications, and how it perpetuates an even deeper level of biblical and theological ignorance.

- **It is not the truth.** "So why is that a problem? In this diverse, relativistic society, what would you expect? After all, who says that your ideas are truth and mine are not? Your problem is that you have a religious (or political/personal/ethnic/socio-economic, etc.) bias against people who do not believe as you do." These sorts of statements and the challenges they present are emblematic of our times. We live in a relativistic age where truth is re-defined depending on the utility that this re-definition may provide anyone at any time. Our world and culture maintain that, "My definition of truth works for me. It may not match your definition of what is truth, but it is my truth. And I'll use it however I want."

May I say that the definition of truth I propose is one that has had wide acceptance since the beginning of Western civilization. It is a simple, ancient one: Truth is the way things really are. And when we deviate from the truth by defining it in our own manner, we cheapen it and sow the seeds of confusion whereby meaningful communication, and thus understanding, are eliminated.

- **Truth matters.** If truth is the way things really are, then we want this truth. It is not a good thing to accept things the way they are not. To do so is to live in a world that is not real, a world that is not rational. In other words, if we shun truth, we are fooling ourselves and have created a self-made fantasyland. As Christians, our standard is, in all things, Christ. And He is in all things the epitome of truthfulness. We cannot experientially and relationally live in a rational world without truth; and without truth, no actual means of communication exists. Truth does matter because it is a necessary foundation for all dimensions of our existence.

What would our society be like if pharmacists lied to their customers? Or if insurance agents tricked clients into signing false contracts? Or if bank loan officers agreed to a certain rate by which to loan money, then later changed the loan rate? What if a car salesman told a potential customer that every element of a particular car is covered by a maintenance warranty, when he knew it did not? We depend on people telling us the truth, and when that does not happen, our lives are in some manner or form disrupted—sometimes with disastrous results.

Likewise, if someone presumes to speak on God's behalf or teach others about the things of God, it must always be done with an unwavering regard for the truth. To fall short of the standard of truth is a grave and dreadful error. To superficially or flippantly disregard what is true is an offense against God. God does not change—He is immutable, meaning that, in accordance with His own nature, He cannot and will not change. Thus, God's truth is the same yesterday, today, and tomorrow. And the truth matters because, as Augustine taught in the 5th century, all truth is God's truth. When our society tries to redefine truth, all we are doing is "kicking against the goads" of God's immutable order.

- **But do all the details matter?** In other words, what if I am 99% right? Isn't that substantially the truth? What about 95%? Or 90%? How much of the truth are we willing to give away before we cross the line into untruth?

There is a real difference between lying and speaking an untruth. Lying is telling an untruth, despite the possession of the truth. Lying is not relaying the truth to someone because of some sort of self-centered motivation—there is in lying a deviousness that is clearly intentional. However, speaking an untruth is done in a state of ignorance. Speaking an untruth does not rest on a motivation of deception, but on a state of ignorance.

But back to the question, how much of the truth is required for it to be considered truth? By definition, the truth must be all true. How pure must water be to be considered pure water? How long must a meter be to be considered a full meter? How many seconds makes up a complete or true minute—55 seconds? 59 seconds? 61 seconds? The comparisons could be endless, but the result must always be the same: there is only one truth, and the details do matter.

- **Compounded untruth.** Consider what happens when less than the truth is tolerated, yet worse when it is promoted. The more a person or an organization tolerates lies or an un-truth, the worse things get. A lie or untruth compounded ultimately results in a situation where the truth is so distant as to be unrecognizable.

A prime example is the Roman Catholic Church. At every doctrinal turn, systemic prevarication results in deeper, more outrageous unbiblical assertions. Consider the case of what Rome has done to the Virgin Mary. At first Mary, the virgin mother of Jesus, was promoted by the church at Rome as being "perpetually a virgin" despite the clear Scriptural evidence to the contrary. Then she had to be immaculately conceived. After that came the doctrine of Mary's "bodily assumption" directly into heaven at her death, in both body and soul (like Jesus). The Roman Church then bestowed upon Mary a unique form of worship called *hyper-dulia*, for she was to be exalted over all other saints. Mary was then given the privilege of acquiring the title of the "Mother of God." Then Marian cultic devotion promoted her into assuming a role (alongside Jesus) as God's co-mediator, a co-mediator alongside Jesus to mediate between the people and God. Now there is a movement in Rome to make her a "co-redeemer"; the next role the Roman magisterium has planned for Mary is that she (and not just Jesus) will be your redeemer. The next time you sing, "I Know That My Redeemer Liveth," you will have to ask yourself, which redeemer? Jesus or Mary? Imagine the heresy and blasphemy!

The result of this and an endlessly growing long string of lies and untruths is "Mariolatry"—a most unbiblical, pagan elevation of Mary that fits the definition of idolatry. And it all started with just a slight departure from the truth, then added more and more untruth. Compounded untruth soon becomes blatant fabrication.

- **Interpreting or applying Scripture outside its context**. The youth pastor in our Prologue used a passage of Scripture to reinforce the lesson he was leading. Remember that his lesson revolved around the idea that life for a modern teenager is hard, but that God loves a person just the way they are—even with all their sin. The passage he cited to substantiate his point was John 16:27. In this verse Jesus says, "for the Father Himself loves you, because you have loved Me and have believed that I came from God."

Every text has a context—a setting. That setting is almost always defined by what comes before and after the text in question. Using a biblical text improperly outside of its context results in error. So when we use a text to make a point, we must insure that the text is used consistent with its original context and the intent of the author and speaker in his time and setting.

In this case in order to assess the meaning of the Bible verse that the youth pastor used (John 16:27), we must examine its context—what is the setting and what is the intent of the author and speaker. Here is a portion of the situation that precedes John 16:27. The passage is John 16:17-26:

> So some of His disciples said to one another, "What is this that He says to us, 'A little while, and you will not see Me, and again a little while, and you will see Me'; and, 'because I am going to the Father'?" So they were saying, "What does He mean by 'a little while'? We do not know what He is talking about." Jesus knew that they wanted to ask Him, so He said to them, "Is this what you are asking yourselves, what I meant

by saying, 'A little while and you will not see Me, and again a little while and you will see Me'? Truly, truly, I say to you, you will weep and lament, but the world will rejoice. You will be sorrowful, but your sorrow will turn into joy. When a woman is giving birth, she has sorrow because her hour has come, but when she has delivered the baby, she no longer remembers the anguish, for joy that a human being has been born into the world. So also you have sorrow now, but I will see you again, and your hearts will rejoice, and no one will take your joy from you. In that day you will ask nothing of Me. Truly, truly, I say to you, whatever you ask of the Father in My name, He will give it to you. Until now you have asked nothing in My name. Ask, and you will receive, that your joy may be full. I have said these things to you in figures of speech. The hour is coming when I will no longer speak to you in figures of speech but will tell you plainly about the Father. In that day you will ask in

My name, and I do not say to you
that I will ask the Father on your
behalf;   (John 16:17-26)

Then comes the focal verse, the verse under
examination, the verse that the youth pastor
used for his example:

for the Father himself loves you,
because you have loved me and
have believed that I came from
God.   (John 16:27)

Then the last part of John Chapter 16
finishes with the following:

I came from the Father and have
come into the world, and now I am
leaving the world and going to the
Father."   His disciples said, "Ah,
now You are speaking plainly and
not using figurative speech! Now
we know that You know all things
and do not need anyone to
question You; this is why we
believe that You came from God."
Jesus answered them, "Do you
now believe? Behold, the hour is
coming, indeed it has come, when
you will be scattered, each to his

own home, and will leave Me alone. Yet I am not alone, for the Father is with Me. I have said these things to you, that in Me you may have peace. In the world you will have tribulation. But take heart; I have overcome the world." (John 16:28-33)

It is quite clear from what comes before and what comes after John 16:27 that this passage has to do with Jesus teaching His close ring of intimate disciples, encouraging them to ask for spiritually beneficial things in His name. And Jesus is informing them that when they do ask, their requests will be honored because they are known and loved by the Father as a result of their love and belief in Jesus.

It is equally clear that it is a misuse, a misapplication of the verse to apply it the way the youth pastor did. Every verse has a context, and every verse can only be rightly used in consideration for that context and the intent of the author and speaker.

When we inadvertently misuse a passage of Scripture it is an untruth. If we know better, and intentionally twist Scripture to say what we want it to say, it is the same as a lie—an intentional deception despite possession of the truth.

- **Half-truths**. It has been said that telling a half truth is no different from telling a complete lie. In other words, if a person possesses full knowledge of a particular subject, teaching, or incident, and they convey to another person only half of that knowledge because it suits their purposes and plans, it is a lie. We have all been in this position. It is difficult to tell the whole truth, when we believe that a truncated truth serves our purposes much better (at least for the moment). We rationalize that a conversation we have had with someone or a note we sent contained "enough" of the story—at least enough of what we want them to know. But a half-truth, because it is told with an intent to deceive, is the same thing as a lie.

A biblical example of just this sort of thing is given to us in 1 Samuel 15, where King Saul of Israel is ordered by God (through the means of the prophet Samuel) to "Now go and strike Amalek and devote to destruction all that they have. Do not spare them, but kill both man and woman, child and infant, ox and sheep, camel and donkey" (v.3). Later, after Saul defeats the Amalekites and wins the battle, Samuel shows up and speaks with Saul:

> And Samuel came to Saul, and Saul said to him, "Blessed be you to the LORD. I have performed the commandment of the LORD." (v.13)

Saul was telling only a half-truth. He had not "performed the commandment of the Lord." He had performed the portion of the Lord's command with which he agreed, but not all of it. He had spared many of the animals he was commanded to destroy, and he had done so to use the animals for sacrifice to the Lord and to increase his own wealth. He even spared the king of the Amalekites, Agag. When he was challenged for his disobedience by Samuel, he sloughs off responsibility onto his people. Saul has been caught in his half-truth, but Samuel is having none of it:

> Why then did you not obey the voice of the LORD? Why did you pounce on the spoil and do what was evil in the sight of the LORD?" And Saul said to Samuel, "I have obeyed the voice of the LORD. I

have gone on the mission on which the LORD sent me. I have brought Agag the king of Amalek, and I have devoted the Amalekites to destruction. But the people took of the spoil, sheep and oxen, the best of the things devoted to destruction, to sacrifice to the LORD your God in Gilgal." And Samuel said, "Has the LORD as great delight in burnt offerings and sacrifices, as in obeying the voice of the LORD? Behold, to obey is better than sacrifice, and to listen than the fat of rams. For rebellion is as the sin of divination, and presumption is as iniquity and idolatry. Because you have rejected the word of the LORD, He has also rejected you from being king." Saul said to Samuel, "I have sinned, for I have transgressed the commandment of the LORD and your words, because I feared the people and obeyed their voice. Now therefore, please pardon my sin and return with me that I may worship the LORD." And Samuel said to Saul, "I will not return with you. For you have rejected the word of the LORD, and the LORD has rejected you from being king over Israel." (vv.19-26)

As Samuel already knew and as Saul was to learn, partial obedience is disobedience, and a half-truth is a whole lie.

Chapter 2:
The Truth

- What is the truth? Before we proceed further, we need a definition of the truth. In our relativistic society, truth is a moving target, with individuals determining for themselves what is true. A Christian does not have such leeway—truth is defined for the believer in Christ. Where do we go to verify what this truth in Christ is? How do we know that all truth is God's truth?

- The truth does exist. First, as Christians, we must assert that the truth does indeed exist. Others have their doubts. They believe that the truth is as numerous as the individuality of every person living. Interestingly, this is the matter that generates a question that Pontius Pilate asked Jesus during His trial leading to the crucifixion. Jesus tells Pilate that "Everyone

28

who is of the truth listens to my voice." And Pilate responds, "What is truth?" seemingly incredulous that ascertaining the truth is even possible. Is attaining or discovering the truth even achievable? Pilate appears to believe that the truth is relative, as does a growing percentage of our 21ˢᵗ century, post-modern society, which believes that truth depends upon a person's perspective or what a person values.

But Jesus is quite clear about what truth is. In John 14:6 Jesus tells us, in one of His great "I am" statements that, "I am the way, the truth, and the life. No one comes to the Father except through Me" (John 14:6). In other words, Jesus is telling us that there is a truth, an objective truth, and that truth is a person—the person of the Lord Jesus Christ.

- Truth is a person. Truth is a person—Jesus. Later in John 17:17 Jesus appeals to the Father to "Sanctify them in the truth; Your word is truth." Jesus, the *logos*, the living word, He is the truth; and the truth is contained in the word of God—in the Scriptures. There is a truth, and it is embodied in Jesus and is manifested and resides in God's word.

- **"....He has spoken to us...."** Hebrews 1:1-4 says:

> Long ago, at many times and in many ways, God spoke to our fathers by the prophets, but in these last days He has spoken to us by His Son, whom He appointed the heir of all things, through whom also He created the world. He is the radiance of the glory of God and the exact imprint of His nature, and He upholds the universe by the word of His power. After making purification for sins, He sat down at the right hand of the Majesty on high, having become as much superior to angels as the name He has inherited is more excellent than theirs.

So if truth is a person, and that person is Jesus, by what method does He give us this truth? Are we to read the Bible closely and imitate what Jesus is modeling for us? Or do others tell us about the effects of Jesus, so that we are convinced to follow Him? Actually, He gives us something much better. He gives us words—human words that we can understand. Hebrews 1 says that

God used to speak to His people through the prophets. But now, in these "last days," He has chosen to speak to us through Jesus, through the recorded witness of Jesus, for He is far more excellent in all ways than even the angels. And since Jesus is the cornerstone and the apostles are the foundation for this living truth (Eph.2:19-21), these human words are the means that God speaks to His people to give them truth.

- Where/How does this Person give us the truth? God "has spoken to us." He has not spoken through a human-enhanced vision, or given us a special new prophecy, nor has He dispatched special prophets to lead us. No, God Himself has spoken to us through His Son, Jesus—the living word— the divine *logos*, that is far better, far more reliable than any human-affirming experience could ever be. In fact, in 2Peter 1:17-21 the Apostle Peter has declared that the strength and power of this living, inspired word is far, far greater than any personal experience, even the first century experience of witnessing the transfiguration of Jesus and hearing the voice from heaven when he says:

For when He received honor and glory from God the Father, and the voice was borne to Him by the Majestic Glory, "This is My beloved Son, with whom I am well pleased," we ourselves heard this very voice borne from heaven, for we were with Him on the holy mountain. And we have something more sure, the prophetic word, to which you will do well to pay attention as to a lamp shining in a dark place, until the day dawns and the morning star rises in your hearts, knowing this first of all, that no prophecy of Scripture comes from someone's own interpretation. For no prophecy was ever produced by the will of man, but men spoke from God as they were carried along by the Holy Spirit.

Can you understand what Peter is saying? He says "we have something more sure" in the word from God—in the word of truth. This word from God that we possess is more sure than any experience. Experiences will come and go, but the word of God stands forever. And the living word tells us that God's revealed word is truth. Jesus prays to the Father in John 17:17, "Sanctify them in the truth, Your word is truth." And this truth is given in human means in communication through the Scriptures.

- So, is the truth accessible? More than ever, in many different ways, and in different media, the Bible is available as never before. And with the information superhighway of the internet, the Scriptures are at our fingertips, and much of it at no cost. There are many excellent translations in literally hundreds of languages and dialects—all making the truth of God's word more accessible than it has ever been. Availability and accessibility for most of the people on the globe is not an obstacle.

- How is the truth of God's word to be used? As we said in Chapter 1, it is to be used consistent with sound hermeneutical practices and always to be interpreted with two primary concerns in mind: (1) the original intent of the author; and (2) a consideration for the context. First, Scripture cannot say what we want it to say. It must say what the original author, "carried along by the Holy Spirit," intended for it to

33

say. And secondly, Scripture must speak consistent with its context. It has been said that "a text without a context is a pretext" to attempt to make something say what it was never intended to say.

Our youth pastor in his brief lesson cited John 16:27 to substantiate his teaching point. In doing so, he disregarded both of our two hermeneutical rules above. He ignored the intent John the Apostle had in conveying Jesus' words to the reader. And the youth pastor also jerked the passage out of context. As we have said in the previous chapter, Jesus is speaking to His intimate disciples in the Upper Room, only hours before His arrest, trial, and execution. He was not speaking to all peoples, pagans and believers; and nowhere in the entire 16th Chapter of John, or the rest of the gospel account of John, or anywhere else in the New Testament does Jesus or anyone else claim that "God loves you just the way you are." The youth pastor drew a false conclusion based on a faulty use of the text.

In John 16:27 Jesus says that "for the Father himself loves you, because you have loved Me and have believed that I came from God." Obviously the verse says that the Father loves the disciples for a reason— "....because you have loved Me [Jesus] and have believed that I came from God." It does not say that the Father loves everyone unconditionally, "just the way you are."

When people misuse the Scriptures, they act as though the Bible is something to be used as their own tool. Actually, they are belittling God's word, in essence saying that the Bible, even though it is the truth of God's own divine word, can be used in any way and for any purpose they want. And in doing so, they are elevating their own concept of truth over God's.

- What is our obligation? The Bible makes clear that the obligation for accurately handling the word of God resides with the teacher/preacher. James 3:1 says, "Not many of you should become teachers, my brothers, for you know that we who teach will be judged with greater strictness." The youth pastor may not know what the truth is. He may be unaware of what the Scriptures say about the subject he purports to teach. If that is the case, he must keep silent, rather than lead others astray. A teacher who teaches wrongly compounds his error, leading other trusting auditors into continuing and perpetuating error. Even slight, seemingly "minor" errors are dangerous because they lead to distancing the people further and further from the truth. And as we have seen, compounded untruth leads the sheep further and further from the safety of the fold and the protection of the shepherd.

The Scriptures are the standard for all faith and practice for a Christian. The Bible is a sacred oracle from God. It is never to be used as some kind of "wax nose" to be shaped into anything we want it to say.

- Tampering with the truth. To tamper with or "adjust" the truth of Scripture is a dangerous thing. The Bible is inerrant, without any mistakes, always true and never false. Therefore, to add to or subtract from the Scriptures, or to ignore it, or elevate the traditions of men over God's word as found in the Bible—all of these practices are violations of divine instructions. Remember, Jesus Himself tells us that the Scriptures are truth itself, sufficient for all faith and practice for a Christian. We have no warrant, no authority to make adjustments to the content nor to alter the usage of Scripture.

The Bible is the sole authority for the church's and the individual Christian's orthodoxy and orthopraxy. All we know about God comes to us through the medium of the Scriptures. As such, no one has the authority to misuse, misquote, or misconstrue the contents of the Bible.

Chapter 3:
Our True Condition

Having established that, first, there is a truth; then second, that the truth can be discovered and should be used rightly, we turn now to evaluating the statement that the youth pastor made at that Friday night gathering in our prologue.

We have already determined that the Bible passage used by the leader was inappropriately applied. Perhaps it was done so intentionally, perhaps not. Now we need to determine whether the conclusion he conveyed to the youth in attendance was indeed correct. Remember his conclusion? He said that:

> But take heart. God has not left you to handle all of life by yourself. God is your great friend.

He will help you through all that you will have to face. Always remember, people, that God loves you. **He loves you just the way you are.** Even with the sin that you are struggling with and all the things you have done wrong, God will never leave you or forsake you. And even though you might be wondering what life is all about, **never forget that God loves you and me and accepts us just the way we are**.

So now, let us turn to the words I have highlighted. Our goal now is to determine whether what the youth pastor has taught, what he concluded from that evening's lesson is indeed true. Does God truly love us just the way we are? Does He accept us in our present condition? Despite all the wrong things we have done, and the hurt we have caused ourselves and others, does God still love us just the way we are?

The True Condition of Every Human.

To these and other related questions, we must examine the true condition of a human being. And to gain such vital information, we must go to the fountainhead of all the truth—the Scriptures. What does the Bible say about our condition? And what does it say about our acceptance by God as a result of that condition?

- Totally depraved. The Bible does not give us a positive picture about the condition of humans in their natural state. In all aspects of his being—in his mind, will, soul, emotions, thoughts, words, and actions, natural man is said to fall far short of the standard established by God.

Scripture says that by nature we are "children of wrath," (Ephesians 2:3) and this means that our first inclination, indeed our first mandatory response to our constituent self, is to do the things that displease God—to sin against God Himself. By nature (based on our inherent make-up) and in all of the aspects by which we are constituted, we fall woefully short of God's standard. Thus, we can theologically assess ourselves and all of the human race (past, present, and future) as being "totally depraved," meaning that all of our characteristic elements (our will, emotions, thoughts, words, and our actions) are corrupt, infected with our sin, and unacceptable to our Lord.

For pagan non-believers this presents no problem. For they do not believe in the the existence of God, and therefore His judgment toward them (they believe) incurs no penalty. But for the believer, this is a hard thing to accept. Most modern Christians have been fed a steady diet of church activities on Sunday with no true doctrinal teaching or preaching. They do not know who God is, who they are, why Jesus went to the cross, or what He achieved when He went there. They do not know the gospel, nor can they possibly explain it to anyone else. In short, they do not know who they are <u>by nature</u>. So to be told according to the Bible that, <u>based on their own nature</u>, they are actually lost sinners bound for hell is a verity impossible to accept—and so they refuse to accept it, even though this teaching is an integral part of God's word.

No part of God's creation can act outside of its nature. Human beings, animals, plants, even inanimate objects must exist and perform in accordance with their nature. A dog can only do dog things because that is its nature. To expect a dog to do what a squirrel does would be ridiculous. There may be some superficial things that make dogs and squirrels similar, but they are by nature different beings—there are distinctly dog things that are not shared with non-dogs. The point is that all things that exist are bounded, or circumscribed by the limits of their nature. To ask a dog to climb trees, store nuts in for the winter, or make baby squirrels is ridiculous. But a dog acting like a dog is actually just confirmation that all beings (even God Himself) act in accordance with their nature.

Now whether we accept that we, as humans, are by nature totally depraved (again, meaning that all aspects of our being are affected by sin) does not matter. Our acceptance of this truth is not required. The Bible asserts that it is true. Just read and understand how the Scriptures portray the true state of all mankind:

- "The LORD saw that the wickedness of man was great in the earth, and that every intention of the thoughts of his heart was only evil continually." (Genesis 6:5)

- ".....the LORD said in His heart, "I will never again curse the ground because of man, for the intention of man's heart is evil from his youth....." (Genesis 8:21)

- "If they sin against You—for there is no one who does not sin—and You are angry with them and give them to an enemy, so that they are carried away captive to the land of the enemy, far off or near," (1Kings 8:46)

- "Behold, I was brought forth in iniquity, and in sin did my mother conceive me." (Psalm 51:5)

- "The wicked are estranged from the womb; they go astray from birth, speaking lies." (Psalm 58:3)

- "Enter not into judgment with Your servant, for no one living is righteous before You." (Psalm 143:2)

- "We have all become like one who is unclean, and all our righteous deeds are like a polluted garment. We all fade like a leaf, and our iniquities, like the wind, take us away." (Isaiah 64:6)

- "Can the Ethiopian change his skin or the leopard his spots? Then also you can do good who are accustomed to do evil?" (Jeremiah 13:23)

- "The heart is deceitful above all things, and desperately sick; who can understand it?" (Jeremiah 17:9)

- "And this is the judgment: the light has come into the world, and people loved the darkness rather than the light because their works were evil." (John 3:19)

- "For the wrath of God is revealed from heaven against all ungodliness and unrighteousness of men, who by their unrighteousness suppress the truth. For what can be known about God is plain to them, because God has shown it to them.
For His invisible attributes, namely, His eternal power and divine nature, have been clearly perceived, ever since the creation of the world, in the things that have been made. So they are without excuse. For although they knew God, they did not honor Him as God or give thanks to him, but they became futile in their thinking, and their foolish hearts were darkened." (Romans 1:18-21)

- "as it is written: none is righteous, no, not one; no one understands; no one seeks for God. All have turned aside; together they have become worthless; no one does good, not even one. Their throat is an open grave; they use their tongues to deceive. The venom of asps is under their lips. Their mouth is full of curses and bitterness.

Their feet are swift to shed blood; in their paths are ruin and misery, and the way of peace they have not known. There is no fear of God before their eyes." (Romans 3:10-18)

- "And you were dead in the trespasses and sins in which you once walked, following the course of this world, following the prince of the power of the air, the spirit that is now at work in the sons of disobedience—among whom we all once lived in the passions of our flesh, carrying out the desires of the body and the mind, and were **by nature children of wrath**, like the rest of mankind." (Ephesians 2:1-3)

- "If we say we have no sin, we deceive ourselves, and the truth is not in us.....If we say we have not sinned, we make Him a liar, and His word is not in us."
(1 John 1:8,10)

The biblical evidence testifying to our depravity is mountainous. It goes on and on. It is as if God anticipates our protests that we are really better than what He is reporting. And, consequently, He buries us under an avalanche of scriptural verification. We are lost; we are sinners; we are the damned. And left to ourselves, as the children of wrath that we are, God is just and righteous to condemn us.

- Children of wrath, but whose wrath?
We are rightly called "children of wrath." But whose wrath is it that is against us? Some clever people try to explain away the source of the wrath as being Satan, or the unbelieving world, or other religions, but the Bible is having none of this nonsense. It is the wrath of God. It is God Himself who is our greatest problem. Jesus reminds us in Matthew 10:28, "And do not fear those who kill the body but cannot kill the soul. Rather fear Him who can destroy both soul and body in hell."

Yes, our biggest problem is God Himself. He is the one who has all power, all knowledge, and is everywhere all at once in His entirety. And it is He whom we have offended and against whom we have rebelled. We have violated all of His standards, all of His commands. And compared to the mountains of sins we have accumulated against ourselves, our repentance is a pitifully weak apology for all that we have done.

- Slaves to sin. We are not only sinners, we are also slaves to sin. Romans 6 makes

46

this abundantly clear. We are slaves to the person or thing we serve and obey—in the case of natural man, that master is sin. This does not mean that we have lost our human free will. When we are slaves to sin, we willingly follow the dictates of our master. Human beings constantly make free will choices, but the issue is not the free will in our choices, but the choices themselves. For while we are a slave to sin, we only make choices that reflect our nature—we only have the ability to make sinful choices.

A person might say, "Well, wait a minute. I helped a little old lady across the street yesterday. Surely that was not a sinful choice." But we must be honest with ourselves—we must sincerely examine our motivations for what we do. When we do that we find many ulterior, self-serving motives—we want to achieve something for ourselves, we want to be perceived by others as being a good or intelligent or nice or handsome or clever person. When we truthfully, sincerely examine our motives, we find that in our natural human state, we are slaves to sin.

- And we are spiritually dead. Because by nature we are totally corrupt and slaves to sin, we are rightly judged to be spiritually dead. We may, for a time, be walking around as if we are alive physically, but we are "dead men walking" because we are assessed as being lawbreakers in God's kingdom— perhaps physically alive for a moment in time, but nevertheless spiritually dead. And let us have no nonsense about being just "morally challenged," or "ethically deprived." And nothing about being just weak or wounded, for the Bible says we are dead— with no spiritual life at all, and no hope of recovery.

People in their natural state, those who have not been born again, are said to be "in the flesh." This is a state of moral corruption, slaves to sin, and spiritually dead. This phrase "in the flesh" occurs twenty-one times in the New Testament, and it refers principally to those who still walk in their human or worldly ways:

- "For while we were living in the flesh, our sinful passions, aroused by the law, were at work in our members to bear fruit for death." (Romans 7:5)

- "For the mind that is set on the flesh is hostile to God, for it does not submit to God's law; indeed, it cannot." (Romans 8:7)

- "Those who are in the flesh cannot please God." (Romans 8:8)

- "But put on the Lord Jesus Christ, and make no provision for the flesh, to gratify its desires." (Romans 13:14)

- "Now the works of the flesh are evident: sexual immorality, impurity, sensuality," (Galatians 5:19)

- "And those who belong to Christ Jesus have crucified the flesh with its passions and desires." (Galatians 5:24)

- "For all that is in the world—the desires of the flesh and the desires of the eyes and pride in possessions—is not from the Father but is from the world." (1 John 2:16)

Contrasted with being in the flesh are those who are "in the spirit," those who have been born again, regenerated to newness of life. Contrasting those who are in the flesh and those in the spirit, the Scriptures conclude the following:

- "in order that the righteous requirement of the law might be fulfilled in us, who walk not according to the flesh but according to

the Spirit. For those who live according to the flesh set their minds on the things of the flesh, but those who live according to the Spirit set their minds on the things of the Spirit. For to set the mind on the flesh is death, but to set the mind on the Spirit is life and peace.........You, however, are not in the flesh but in the Spirit, if in fact the Spirit of God dwells in you. Anyone who does not have the Spirit of Christ does not belong to Him. But if Christ is in you, although the body is dead because of sin, the Spirit is life because of righteousness......For if you live according to the flesh you will die, but if by the Spirit you put to death the deeds of the body, you will live. For all who are led by the Spirit of God are sons of God."
(Romans 8:4-6,9-10, 13-14)

    - "For the desires of the flesh are against the Spirit, and the desires of the Spirit are against the flesh, for these are opposed to each other, to keep you from doing the things you want to do." (Galatians 5:17)

    - "For the one who sows to his own flesh will from the flesh reap corruption, but the one who sows to the Spirit will from the Spirit reap eternal life." (Galatians 6:8)

- ".....for whatever does not proceed from faith is sin." (Romans 14:23)

- And thus, humans are, by nature, God's enemies. Reflect on the human situation for a moment: we are <u>by nature</u> totally depraved, a child of wrath, a slave to sin, and spiritually dead. In our natural state, we can do nothing to please God. The result is that, as the Bible says, we are God's enemy.

For many professing Christians, this is just not possible. God cannot possibly see humans as children of wrath. He cannot possibly see us as rebels, lawbreakers, and His enemies. It is incomprehensible to many uninformed Christians that God would see human beings in any other way than as an object of His limitless and unfailing love. And why do they believe this? Because they are more comfortable in their pseudo-Christian tradition than they are with the truths found in the Scriptures. They want to insulate themselves from the truth in the false lessons and bad theology that have been perpetrated upon most modern-day Christians, rather than finding out and living out the truth.

One of the hard truths of the Bible is that in our natural state, we humans are enemies of God. Romans 5:10 says, "For if while we were enemies we were reconciled to God by the death of his Son, much more, now that we are reconciled, shall we be saved by his life." The Apostle Paul also reminds us in Romans 8:7 that, "For the mind that is set on the flesh is hostile to God, for it does not submit to God's law; indeed, it cannot." In Colossians 1:21 Paul teaches us that we are "alienated and hostile in mind, doing evil deeds" against God.

And human worldliness is also an identification of hostility toward God. As James writes in chapter 4, verse 4:

> You adulterous people! Do you not know that friendship with the world is enmity with God? Therefore whoever wishes to be a friend of the world makes himself an enemy of God.

And continuing the idea that those who are of the world are enemies of God, the Apostle John writes in 1 John 2:15-16:

> Do not love the world or the things in the world. If anyone loves the world, the love of the Father is not in him. For all that is in the world—

the desires of the flesh and the desires of the eyes and pride in possessions—is not from the Father but is from the world.

So in our natural state, in our human nature, we are the enemies of God, fighting against His purposes and subject to His unmitigated wrath. And because of the evil and malice of the devil, the world, our flesh, and our own hearts, we are justly and rightly condemned by God. And as George Whitefield (1714-1770) reminded us in one of his most famous sermons, "The Method of Grace":

> We can do no good thing *by nature*: 'They that are in the flesh cannot please God.' You may do things materially good, but you cannot do a thing formally and rightly good; *because nature cannot act above itself.* It is impossible that a man who is unconverted can act for the glory of God; he cannot do anything in faith, and 'whatsoever is not of faith is sin.'

In Romans 3:10-12,16-18, the Apostle Paul repeats the judgment found in the Old

53

Testament that humans are rightly convicted of their rebellion and lawlessness against God:

> .... None is righteous, no, not one; no one understands; no one seeks for God. All have turned aside; together they have become worthless; no one does good, not even one....... in their paths are ruin and misery, and the way of peace they have not known. There is no fear of God before their eyes.

And So ....

Having examined what the Bible says about the human condition, and having recognized that we are children of wrath, that we are God's enemies, and that in our natural state we are spiritually dead and cannot do anything rightly good, what are we to do? How can we exist as God's enemy? How are we to cope knowing that our fate is our own destruction? That we cannot have true peace in our hearts? First, we must have a right assessment of ourselves. We must acknowledge the truth of the Bible when it tells us that we are sinners, law-breakers, and adversaries of God. Once we come to terms with that, we can begin to have a right appraisal of our incredibly dire, indeed, impossible situation.

- We must admit that we are self-centered and self-absorbed. Part of our problem is that our words/thoughts/actions are all focused on ourselves. Such an outlook is revealed through our fallen human nature. This is dreadfully unfortunate, for it clouds our minds with an appraisal of ourselves that is not reflective of who we are as portrayed in the Scriptures. Instead, we must see ourselves as God sees us. To see ourselves any other way is an exercise in self-deception.

- We must use the standard of Scripture to assess ourselves. If the Bible is the word of God (and it is) it must be the sole standard by which our nature and actions are judged. And the Bible must be the sole authority for the right assessment of who we are—just the Bible, not our traditions, not our shared ignorance, nor our misplaced emotionalism. Like a spoiled child, we have frequently been told and taught what we have wanted to hear. But we must begin to act like "grown-ups" and "put away childish things." And when this happens we will see that we are so far short of the righteousness that is required, we have inherently no hope within ourselves.

- So does God love us just the way we are? God love us the way we are? No, of course not**. He hates us the way we are**. He detests sin, and He sees that in our human nature we are slaves to sin and our evil desires. He hates what we have become. And He insists, He demands that we be changed.

- How do we know this is right? So how do we know that God demands that we be changed? How can we be sure that we are unacceptable in our human nature? Because the Father, took the incredibly miraculous step of sending His Son to the earth in the form of a human being. Because He sent a mighty savior to redeem us from ourselves. Because at an infinitely high cost, the death of His Son, He accomplished a plan to redeem the souls of all those for whom Christ would die, rescuing them from eternal separation from the Father's love and condemnation in eternal torment. Jesus Christ is the reason that we recognize that God hates us the way we are, and yet He is

<u>also the proof that **_He loves us too much to leave us the way we are_**</u>.

Chapter 4:
The Bad News and the Good News

This general condition of ignorance of most evangelicals about the true condition of humanity is reflected, more than anywhere else, in how the gospel message is viewed. Because evangelicals and most other Christians are badly misinformed about the condition of mankind, they are equally deficient of any understanding about the gospel.

The gospel is the "good news" of God's plan, based solely on His grace, for redeeming a people from the fate that all humans deserve—an eternity of torment separated from the love of God. But the good news is only good news if first you understand what the bad news is.

- The bad news, then the good news.
Imagine if, as your friend, I came up to you and told you that you must take a wonderful new medicine I had developed. I explained that this medicine, with only a few minor side-effects, can not only prevent cancer in the body, but it can also completely reverse the effects of cancer where it appears and do so for the rest of a person's lifetime. You might hail my discovery and manufacture of such a drug, and congratulate me on my success, but your enthusiasm for the medicine would have its limits. And certainly you would not feel compelled to take the medicine yourself just because your friend had developed it and then told you about it.

But imagine a different scenario. What if I had first come to you and told you that I had just come from your physician's office. He told me, as one doctor to another, that you were dying of cancer, and that the recent battery of tests he had administered to you confirmed that the ravenous killing cells had spread throughout your body. You only had a few months to live, only time to put your personal affairs in order before your imminent death. But then I announced to you my breakthrough with a new medicine that had the proven ability to prevent and eliminate cancer. Suddenly, there was hope, there was joyous enthusiasm for my drug. Where before there was only a passing interest in the professional success of a friend, now there was personal involvement, personal passion, and jubilation at the prospect of the potential for relief—even a kind of rebirth.

What caused the difference in the two scenarios? The information of the new medicine was the same; and my professional success was the same. But I would submit to you that what made the good news of the cure so good was the level of badness of the bad news. You see, in my first scenario there was no bad news really. Oh sure, you understood that *some* people in the world get cancer, and *some* people out there even die from the disease; but until a person determines that the information about cancer is bad (i.e., that <u>you</u> have the disease), then the good news about the medicine is not really that good. You see, my dear reader, what makes the good news good is first hearing and understanding the bad news.

The gospel is the same way. Without the knowledge and understanding of the bad news of our natural human condition, there really is no good news contained in the gospel. Until a person first sees himself and believes himself to be a lost and dying sinner, condemned to an eternity in hell, with no reprieve and no hope—until then and only then, the gospel will seem to be an interesting story to him, but only a story. Oh, but once the scales fall from the condemned man's eyes, once the Spirit replaces his heart of stone with a circumcised heart of flesh, once he has by the power of God been born again, and sees his true condition as God sees it, then the gospel becomes the sweetest news possible. You see, the bad news makes the good news good.

- Telling the bad news first. This is why when we share our faith with another person, we must be truthful and first tell them the bad news about their actual condition in the eyes of a holy God—a God who has all power, knows all things, and exist in His entirety everywhere. We must tell them that they may seem to be alright on the outside, and their personal conditions may even seem to be somewhat agreeable, but on the inside, they are, as Jesus said to the self-righteous Pharisees, "....you are like whitewashed tombs, which outwardly appear beautiful, but within are full of dead

people's bones and all uncleanness."
(Matthew 23:37)

- **In order to make the good news indispensible.** We do not tell people about the dangers of their nature and their sin in order to frighten, nor to afflict them, nor to cause them to hustle on over to their nearest neighborhood church. We tell them the truth so that they realize their true condition, which will give them a context for understanding the gospel. We ought to pursue and to use the truth, and then to tell the whole truth so that the gospel can be for the lost what it has always been— indispensible. Anything else is a dereliction of our duty as ambassadors for Christ.

- **God Himself is the gospel.** Not only do we tell the truth, we also insure that we do not convolute or complicate the gospel. A frequent error in relating the gospel is that we confuse the *benefits* of the gospel with the gospel itself. For example, eternal life is not the gospel. Eternal life is a trait of all humans that are born—either eternal life in heaven in the presence of God, or eternal life in hell separated from the love of God. But eternal life with God is not the gospel; it is a benefit of the gospel. Likewise, living in heaven forever, being adopted into God's family, living in a glorified body in a place that has no more tears or sorrow—all of this is a benefit of the gospel, but not the gospel itself.

When we confuse the benefits of the gospel with the essence of the gospel itself, we demonstrate that we do not understand what God has revealed to us in His eternal, cosmic plan; nor do we understand the cost of the gospel to God Himself. In fact, when all we talk and think about concerning the gospel are its benefits, we cheapen the value and divine intent of all that is accomplished in the gospel.

Instead, what we should realize and proclaim about the gospel (the plan of God for redeeming His elect people set in motion even before there was a creation) is what John Piper explained so eloquently in his book, *God Is the Gospel*. And that is the point. God is the gospel; <u>God Himself</u> is the Gospel. He is the "good news" of and for our salvation. As Piper so compellingly says:

> Our fatal error is believing that wanting to be happy means wanting to be made much of. It feels so good to be affirmed. But the good feeling is finally rooted in the worth of self,

not the worth of God. This path to happiness is an illusion.....The sad thing is that a radically man-centered view of love permeates our culture and our churches. From the time they can toddle we teach our children that feeling loved means feeling made much of.....But when you apply this definition of love to God, it weakens His worth, undermines His goodness, and steals our satisfaction. If the enjoyment of God Himself is not the final and best gift of love, then God is not the greatest treasure, His self-giving is not the highest mercy, the gospel is not the good news that sinners may enjoy their Maker, Christ did not suffer to bring us to God, and our souls must look beyond Him for satisfaction....We are willing to be God-centered, it seems, as long as God is man-centered. We are willing to boast in the cross as long as the cross is a witness to our worth. Who then is our pride and joy? ..... The good news is not that there is no pain or death or sin or hell. There is. The good news is that the King Himself has come, and these enemies have been defeated, and if we trust in what He has done and what He promises, we will escape the death sentence and see the glory of our Liberator and live with Him forever.

Chapter 5:
Keeping the Gospel Message From the People

Unbelievably, what we find is that the true gospel has been intentionally hidden from the people. Most in the Christian world have not heard the true gospel message as conveyed in the Scriptures.

- Why is the truth of the gospel hidden from the people? The question must be posed and answered. Why is the true gospel not given to the people? Note that I do not surmise that the gospel has been inadvertently misplaced or mistakenly edited out of the Scriptures. There is an intentionality about keeping the Christian gospel message from the people.

Certainly, in this matter, individual Christian believers are not completely innocent victims. Their apathy, lack of Christian discipline, weak commitment to their faith, and their willingness to abdicate their individual responsibility to pursue the truth found in Scripture are unquestionably contributing factors to the state of the gospel found in the church today.

But, as we shall see, the leaders of the church must shoulder the greater responsibility for this deplorable state of affairs—this willful hiding of the true gospel.

- **A history.** There is a history of keeping the gospel from the people. During the era of the medieval church, a number of highly destructive influences worked to separate the people of Christ from the truth of the gospel: (1) the rise of the alleged infallible papacy; (2) the unbiblical codification of a Roman priestcraft; (3) the sacerdotal emphasis of the church; (4) the advent of institutional monasticism; (5) the Roman church's insistence in the sole use of the Latin Vulgate Bible; and (6) the overall drift away from the authority of the Bible (vis-à-vis church tradition and the teachings of the church magisterium). These and other highly negative influences have worked against the teaching of the gospel message.

- Why the deception? Why indeed! Why does anyone do something that is opposed to the purposes of God? Human nature; greed for money or power or prestige; ignorance; and an assortment of motives too numerous to mention. Just because a person becomes a church leader does not absolve them from the human motivations inherent in their fallen nature. For a reminder of this we turn back to the wise words of the previously cited Whitefield sermon, "The Method of Grace":

> As God can send a nation or people no greater blessing than to give them faithful, sincere, and upright ministers, so the greatest curse that God can possibly send upon a people in this world, is to give them over to blind, unregenerate, carnal, lukewarm, and unskilled guides. And yet, in all ages, we find that there have been many wolves in sheep's clothing, many that daubed with untempered mortar, that prophesied smoother things than God did allow. As it was formerly, so

it is now; there are many that corrupt the Word of God and deal deceitfully with it. It was so in a special manner in the prophet Jeremiah's time; and he, faithful to his Lord, faithful to that God who employed him, did not fail from time to time to open his mouth against them, and to bear a noble testimony to the honor of that God in whose name he from time to time spake. If you will read this prophecy, you will find that none spake more against such ministers than Jeremiah, and here especially in the chapter out of which the text is taken (Jeremiah 6), he speaks very severely against them—he charges them with several crimes; particularly, he charges them with covetousness: "For," says he in the 13th verse, "from the least of them even to the greatest of them, everyone is given to covetousness; and from the prophet even unto the priest, every one dealeth false." And then, in the words of the text, in a more special manner, he exemplifies how they had dealt falsely, how they had behaved treacherously to poor souls: says he, "They have healed also the hurt of the daughter of my people slightly, saying, 'Peace, peace,' when there is no peace"...... The prophet gives a thundering message, that they might be terrified and have some convictions and inclinations to repent; but it seems that the false prophets, the false priests, went about stifling people's convictions, and when they were hurt or a little terrified, they were for daubing over the wound, telling them that Jeremiah was but an enthusiastic preacher, that there could be no such thing as war among them, and saying to people, 'Peace, peace, be still,' when the prophet told them there was no peace.

- Left to the leadership of "blind, unregenerate, carnal, lukewarm, and unskilled guides." In Matthew 15:14 Jesus, speaking about the Pharisees, says, "Let them alone; they are blind guides. And if the blind lead the blind, both will fall into a pit." Is this not the state of the evangelical church today in far too many instances? The leadership is, in innumerable instances, "blind, unregenerate, carnal, lukewarm, and unskilled." Therefore, the congregants are without true biblical leadership. And if the leaders are not following the precepts of Scripture, what hope have the people to avoid the pit?

- Ignorant, clueless, and sold out to the world. In far too many cases, evangelical churches are being led by those who are deficient in their knowledge of Scripture, the gospel, church history, and other religions of the world. These church leaders, therefore, have no biblical or intellectual context through which they ought to rightly teach their people. They are the blind leading the blind and are repeatedly teaching and preaching "a different gospel." Because they are ignorant of Scripture, they fall back upon what they are most comfortable—the world and its intellectually and biblically bankrupt philosophies. They are most likely to see the church and its people as a business and themselves as the CEO. Their own style is to try to rely upon the world's methodologies for organizing the activities of the church, figuring that what works well in the world can also be transferred to the church.

71

But the church is not to be like the world. The church is comprised of "saints." The word saint comes from the Greek word ἅγιοι that is transliterated "hagioi" and means the holy, sanctified, or separated ones. And from what are these saints sanctified or separated? Why, from the world, of course. God Himself calls out a people to be His own, for His own purposes. Paul reminds us of this when he writes in Romans 8:30 about those whom God elects, "And those whom he predestined He also called, and those whom He called He also justified, and those whom He justified He also glorified." It is clear that He has a particular plan for the saints whom He separates out of the world.

And Paul, by clear implication of this plan, gives the believer, the saint, some practical advice in living out the Christian life:

> Do not be unequally yoked with unbelievers. For what partnership has righteousness with lawlessness? Or what fellowship has light with darkness? What accord has Christ with Belial? Or what portion does a believer share with an unbeliever? What agreement has the temple of

God with idols? For we are the temple of the living God; as God said, "I will make My dwelling among them and walk among them, and I will be their God, and they shall be My people. Therefore go out from their midst, and be separate from them," says the Lord, "and touch no unclean thing; then I will welcome you, and I will be a Father to you, and you shall be sons and daughters to Me," says the Lord Almighty. (2 Corinthians 6:14-18)

So why would any pastor, elder, or church leader attempt to promote the world's techniques and practices within the church, when it is those very activities and motivations from which the church is called to be separated? It can only be explained by either gross ignorance of God's word or an unwarranted, treasonous infatuation with the world—both of which are catastrophic for the well-being of any church body.

- Biblical ignorance. The most damaging and most perplexing phenomenon is the ignorance of the Bible by those who claim to be leaders in "Bible-believing" churches. As the supreme authority for the church in matters of Christian faith and practice, the Bible must be a central focus for discerning God's will for His church and should be the instrument by which the church is organized, operated, and educated. We have access to more methods to learn the Bible and more translations available to us than at any time in the history of the human race. Yet many evangelical leaders and their congregants remain woefully ignorant of its central themes and the hermeneutical principles involved in serious Bible study.

In the book of Romans the Apostle Paul expresses his concern for the welfare and salvation of his people, the people of Israel. He notes that their problem is not that they have failed to be enthusiastic or "zealous" for the things of God, writing, "For I bear them witness that they have a zeal for God, but not according to knowledge" (Romans 10:2). Oh yes, they were hard after the things of God, but it was based on an insufficient knowledge of God and what He required.

And it was not an innocent ignorance, but one that led to dire consequences. "For, being ignorant of the righteousness of God, and seeking to establish their own, they did not submit to God's righteousness" (Romans 10:3). In other words, because of their ignorance of the word of God and what He desired, they did not submit to God and were to find themselves rebelling against God and His Messiah. All out of their ignorance—they had zeal, but it was an ignorant zeal.

- What we have is a failure to communicate. We have a fundamental misunderstanding about the nature of God. He does not exist to make us happy. And yet this is what many Christians are told about God and the Christian faith. "Just accept Jesus and make Him the lord of your life, and everything will go much better for you." Some notable people make a living (and end up writing *New York Times* bestsellers about it) telling people that God is just waiting to do all He can to make your life the heaven it was intended to be—*Your Best Life Now*, so to speak. Such a notion has no foundation in the Bible—but only in the hearts of fallen men.

The fact is that after a person becomes a Christian, their life may truly become more difficult; not easier, but harder. In the case of "the disappointed Christian" who has been taught that God is at his beck and call and will make his life more bearable, many things may go wrong (at least from the perspective of the world) after his conversion. Despite the false counsel of the word-faith teachers, these purveyors of the "prosperity gospel," the life of a new believer (or an old one for that matter) may get far worse than expected. In fact, suffering seems to be an essential aspect of becoming a Christian. It certainly was for the early believers, as Luke writes:

> ....and when they had called in the apostles, they beat them and charged them not to speak in the name of Jesus, and let them go. Then they left the presence of the council, rejoicing that they were counted worthy to suffer dishonor for the name [of Jesus]. (Acts 5:40-41)

Paul says in Philippians 1:29, "For it has been granted to you on behalf of Christ not only to believe on Him, but also to suffer for Him."

And Peter reminds the scattered believers of the 1st century in Asia Minor:

> Beloved, do not be surprised at the fiery trial when it comes upon you to test you, as though something

strange were happening to you. But rejoice insofar as you share Christ's sufferings, that you may also rejoice and be glad when his glory is revealed. (1 Peter 4:12-13)

So suffering with and for Christ is part of the Christian life. But the blind guides who lead people astray want this to remain hidden from the people. The reasoning is that if anyone would get wind that suffering is a constituent part of what it means to be a Christian, there would be fewer Christians.

But this kind of worldly thinking ignores the sovereignty of God. It only exposes the false teachers for who they truly are—the blind leading the blind. After all, those whom God decides to save will, in the end, be saved. It is part of His "irresistible grace." So the truth of the gospel and the "fellowship of suffering" with Jesus Christ will only chase away those who will never be saved anyway.

- Does it really matter what we believe? Don't all beliefs lead to God?
There is an undergirding trust, even among people who claim to be Christians, that there are many ways to heaven, many ways to receive salvation from God. Despite the

words of Jesus in John 14:6 ("....I am *the* way, *the* truth, and *the* life. No one comes to the Father but through Me."), many believe there are diverse ways to receive salvation and eternal life. Their assertion is that as long as a person is sincere and genuine in their personal faith, their religion can lead them to God. But this is clearly not consistent with Scripture.

This false belief is designed to avoid the most heinous of all faults in a post-modern world—that of being accused of being intolerant. But the Bible is having none of this nonsense. Christ is the only way to be regenerated and made acceptable to God; Christ's work alone can save us; and there is only one God who saves. This is a very exclusive salvation. We might say that God is a very intolerant God. And despite what the false teachers and preachers say, we are not acceptable to Him "just the way we are"—the way we naturally are is definitely, biblically quite unacceptable.

- Osteen: "do not mention sin." Lest a person might believe that this is a minor, insignificant issue, one need only to look at the largest "church" in the country today—Lakewood Church in Houston, Texas—to understand the extent of the problem. In a

78

famous interview with television host Larry King of CNN on June 20, 2005, the pastor of Lakewood Church, Joel Osteen, said the following about sin:

> KING: You don't call them sinners?
> OSTEEN: I don't.
> KING: Is that a word you don't use?
> OSTEEN: I don't use it. I never thought about it. But I probably don't. But most people already know what they're doing wrong. When I get them to church I want to tell them that you can change. There can be a difference in your life. So I don't go down the road of condemning.

Despite the fact that the word "sin" is used over 800 times in the Scriptures, Joel Osteen admits in the interview and in subsequent sermons and interviews that he does not use the word "sin" because of its negative effect on the 37,000 people who attend Lakewood on any given week. If sin is not important, then who needs a savior? Who needs the gospel or Jesus?

Osteen, a prime example of the word-faith movement spewing a "prosperity gospel" kind of message, is a preacher who has never received any theological training of any sort, and appears to be proud of it. Unbelievably, in his sermons and speeches he does not mention sin. But sin is what causes us to be judged to be "children of wrath." Sin is what separates people from God. Sin is what sends people to hell. And yet Osteen has no use for it in his vocabulary. This is truly a classic case of wanting to create one's own reality, regardless of what the Scriptures say. The words of Paul in Romans 10:2-3 never rang so true. Read them again, for while they were originally intended to describe the Israelites of Paul's day, their truths clearly apply to the case of Mr. Osteen at Lakewood Church:

> For I bear them witness that they have a zeal for God, but not according to knowledge. For, being ignorant of the righteousness of God, and seeking to establish their own, they did not submit to God's righteousness.

- **"All is well" or is it?** Recently I attended a Christmas concert at a nearby mega-church. It was a beautiful production, with hundreds of choir members in tuxedoes and formal dresses, a full orchestra, live animals including elephants and camels, and a Santa Claus in a sleigh that "flew" onto the stage from the rafters. It was an incredible production that rivaled any performance I had seen. And there was a message through the drama portion that even suggested that salvation comes from the gospel of Jesus Christ. The final portion of the performance was a re-creation of the crucifixion of Jesus and His resurrection.

But then the pastor of the church came out to speak to the audience with a single message that he repeated over and over with a smile ..... "All is well." Giving him the benefit of interpreting his words biblically, we might say that he meant that God was in control of all things, but that is not what he apparently meant. He went on to say essentially that it is Christmas time, families are getting together to celebrate, and because God has it all under control, we ought to understand and feel that "All is well."

And while he was technically right in what he said, I was very disappointed with his message. It was sort of a "Joel Osteen light" message. It is true that God has all things under His control, but he was wrong when he said that "all is well." All is not

81

well. Sin abounds on the earth, and in the hearts of too many of God's creatures. All is not well. What God says is evil, too many men say it is good. And what God tells us is good, too many tell us is evil. There is rampant rebellion in the land. All is not well. The pastor had an opportunity to tell the truth, and instead he passed over it to deliver some cotton candy. In effect, he took the course that the false teachers and leaders of Jeremiah's day did, saying, "'Peace, peace,' when there is no peace."

A half truth is a lie and an attempt to deceive, and missing a chance to tell the truth is always a tragedy.

- "Salvation is something that awes us, and doctrine is something that confuses us." About three years ago a mega-church minister in my area presented a sermon that was designed to explain the difference between reformed theology and non-reformed theology. He started the sermon by making the statement that, "Salvation is something that awes us, and doctrine is something that confuses us." And then he spent the rest of the sermon demonstrating that he understood neither reformed theology nor its counterpoint. He might as well have said, "We're really happy that God is going to save us all, but it's too bad that you're too stupid to understand it." But wait a minute. Isn't salvation doctrine? When we talk about salvation, or Jesus, or heaven or hell, we are talking about doctrine. And if doctrine "confuses us," isn't that a reflection of the leadership provided? I suppose if the pastor was honest he could have reworded his opening by saying, "Salvation is something that awes us, but because of my incompetence, and my unwillingness and inability to teach you, you will have to remain ignorant of doctrine." It is this attitude about doctrine that is so condescending and debilitating and that damages the spiritual maturity of the congregation and keeps the true gospel from the people. And unfortunately, this sort of thinking is far too prevalent in the modern evangelical church.

- "Deeds not creeds." This is the mantra of the "progressive" evangelicals that say that at the heart of Christianity, it is not what you believe that is important, but what you actually do. By their metric, being a Mormon is just fine, because they do a lot of "wonderful" things. Only problem is that the Mormons do not believe in the God of the Bible, nor do they have a biblical view of who

Jesus or the Holy Spirit are, and who man is. Additionally, their doctrine of salvation is based on a works-based righteousness. But, by golly, for the "deeds not creeds" crowd, those Mormons sure do some good things!

This is the kind of muddle-headed thinking that is destroying the fabric of the evangelical church. Jesus was continually teaching His disciples that the intent of the heart was the most important factor in whatever they did. And their intent, their motivation for what they did was based on what they believed. When their minds (and their priorities) were fixated on the physical world, they were not receiving the message that Jesus was preaching and teaching. You might say that their "deeds" were affected by their faulty "creeds." That is always the case. It remains true today. The "deeds, not creeds" leadership will therefore always lead the evangelical church into the abyss of biblical heresy.

- Sold out to the world's techniques. Those who would keep the true gospel message from the people do so because they value the methods of the world more than the methods of God. They see that people in the world run after events, games, entertainment venues, sports, and a myriad of other things that cause people to gather in large numbers. So they figure, why not do these things in the church? Why not adopt and adapt the world's methods to cause people to gather in God's church? Such leaders have more faith and belief in the techniques of the world than in the clear message given in the Bible. When the Bible says, "Preach the word," (2Timothy 4:2) they believe they have a better idea. When the Bible says that, "faith comes from hearing, and hearing through the word of Christ" (Romans 10:17), these leaders substitute their own beliefs and their own methods—essentially, they have demonstrated by their prized worldly "methods" that they either: (1) do not believe that the Bible is the word of God; or (2) they believe they are smarter than God is. In either case, they prove themselves to be blind guides unworthy of the trust given them.

- Organized to fail. In its pursuit to copy the world, the modern church has organized for its own failure. The church has seen that the world "pigeon-holes" people by age and circumstances, so for them this seems a good idea for the church. As a result, the church organizes Bible study training by age groups, marital status, and other artificial categories.

Segregating the youth from seniors, the singles from the marrieds, and upon other worldly criteria may seem reasonable to a local church body that is determined to copy the world, but it is without biblical basis. Just like Paul's criticism of the factionalism and misuse of spiritual gifts in the Corinthian church, many of our modern church leaders are seemingly bent upon unnecessarily dividing the congregation into pockets of competing cliques. These become "compartmentalized congregations" that limit interaction and support, producing relationally inept local churches who divide over petty issues instead of uniting through the proclamation of the pure gospel message.

Can it be that the youth of a church have nothing to learn from the adults—to the point that they have to be segregated into a special group? And have the youth nothing to offer the senior members to the point that the senior group will many times exist as a "church within a church"? Can this be the unity the apostles preached about so vehemently to the early church? A church leader who allows this sort of misguided, worldly practice within a church for which he has oversight has fallen under the influence of the world and forsaken the teachings of the apostles.

- Our self-importance and personal esteem are our standard. Whereas the principal focus of the church must be the Lord Jesus Christ, the truth is that the modern evangelical church is organized to please the people in the church. The reasoning goes something like this: (1) bigger is always better (at least that is what the world teaches us); (2) to get bigger we have to focus on the things that people want (that is, mirror the world), not what Scriptures says they need; (3) we must have a lot of people in the local church to pay for the things that they want, so they will keep coming; and (4) therefore, our supreme focus must be on pleasing people, rather than pleasing God.

Like the pagan ancient Greeks, the slogan essentially becomes *homo mensura*— "man is the measure of all things." Man, not God, reigns over all creation and makes all decisions based on his priorities. In other words, all things revolve around man. In the church we are intent upon sacrificing our relationship with God through His word and the leadership of the Spirit (who always perfectly confirms the word) for a very poor substitute—humans.

The modern evangelical church is far more man-centered than it is committed to the glory and worship of our Creator. This is how we slip into the teaching (without provoking even a ripple of protest) that says, "God loves you just the way you are."

- Radically contagious. The cost of all this confusion, all the false teaching, and all the man-centered emphasis is quite a high price to pay. It results in a church characterized by false conversions, an unregenerate church body, a lack of priority upon those things which God says are to be prioritized, and a low opinion of the sovereign God of the universe—the God who made us and saved us from ourselves. Reverend John Sartelle, senior minister of Tates Creek Presbyterian Church in Lexington, Kentucky, has written a brilliant article that succinctly describes the condition in which the modern church finds itself:

> I have always been leery of vaccinations. The idea that bits of a serious disease are put into my body is disconcerting.....The medical explanation is that I am being exposed to weak or dead elements of

the disease so that my body will build the antibodies to combat the sickness. The vaccination makes me immune to the real disease.....That is what has happened with many Christians and churches. They have been vaccinated with dead or weak forms of Christianity. Thus, they have built up antibodies that combat the powerful, radical contagion of authentic Christianity. They are going through the motions of being Christian, but their lives show none of the severe symptoms of true Christianity.......Many churches are no more than inoculation clinics run by the world and Satan. People go there to receive weekly vaccinations, so they won't come down with the real thing.

Sartelle goes on to say that the world need never fear the person who has only had a vaccination of Christianity because, "They can live next to them for years without any fear of catching the virulent strain of the true Christ." But Jesus has called us to be radically contagious Christians armed with the true gospel message of salvation—not just with a weak, unbiblical, man-centered copy of the real thing.

- Finally, Satan blinds us to the truth. Surely our flesh and the world work against the church and its mission. But when the church struggles, as it is today, we should have no doubt that its old adversary, Satan, will be close by. So when we consider the reasons that cause the gospel not to be promulgated among the Lord's people, we must not forget about Satan. Indeed, he is a great enemy of the gospel. As John Piper reminds us in his brilliant book, *God Is the Gospel*:

> Satan is not mainly interested in causing us misery. He is mainly interested in making Christ look bad. He hates Christ. And he hates the glory of Christ. He will do all he can to keep people from seeing Christ as glorious. The gospel is God's instrument for liberating people from exulting in self to exulting in Christ. Therefore Satan hates the gospel.

Chapter 6
How Then Shall We Live?

If, as Piper reminds us, the gospel is the tool of liberation for God's people, how then shall we live? What shall we do? What are we to believe and how shall we act? To whom shall we turn? How ought we to turn loose this instrument of liberation that meets our biblical mandate?

- What should we be teaching (and believing)?   We are to be teaching the truth as revealed to us in Scripture. The truth, and nothing but the truth, so help us God. There is a truth, an objective truth. In the words of Jesus, "....Thy word is truth"

(John 17:17). The truth of the gospel is revealed in the Bible.

- What is this gospel from God? To His human creation, I believe the gospel of the New Covenant can be described in four simple points (though there is much contained within each point):

1. God is holy.
2. Man is not holy.
3. But Jesus was sent to redeem sinners.
4. All those who call upon the name of the Lord will be saved.

And this is also a gospel that applies to all of creation. For the Scriptures say that when the work of the gospel is fully consummated, all things will be made new. All of creation will then experience the gospel in its fullest sense. For although this gospel relates to us humans in a personal and a particularly salvific manner, there is far more at stake than just the salvation of humans. All of creation, all aspects of God's creative power in His vast universe, groans in anticipation of the fullness of time, when all things, by the power of the gospel, will be made new (Romans 8:18-23; Revelation 21:1-5).

As a result, the gospel is fully and rightly comprehended when it is seen and understood as God's message to all of His creation. His human creatures play a central, but not a singular part in the promulgation and consummation of His gospel plan for the ages. And we human teachers of the gospel would do well to teach it properly by instructing our students about the full dimensions of the Lord's plan for redeeming all that He has made.

- We have a mandate to proclaim it. The Bible makes clear that God's people have a mandate to proclaim the gospel to all creation. This is not an optional program, nor can it be avoided by claiming that, "Well, evangelism is not one of my spiritual gifts." Or by telling our people that, "Salvation awes us, but doctrine confuses us." Such fuzzy-headed thinking will not do.

Many Christians draw their principal biblical mandate for evangelism from Jesus' words in Matthew 28:18-20, known as "The Great Commission." While His words are direct and imperative, His words were specifically and directly delivered to the eleven disciples He spoke to after His resurrection. And they performed their given mission magnificently. But depending

93

upon a person's hermeneutic, I believe that the argument that Jesus was speaking to all believers for all time may be problematic.

Rather, I believe our evangelism mandate comes from the words of Paul in Romans 10:9-17. I do so because Paul was speaking to a church, a church like the ones of today that, as believers, we are called to populate. He says that faith comes from the word of Christ, and how can this word be conveyed unless someone goes and tells them? This commission is clearly to us, the church, the believers. We are not 1st century apostles with a direct commission from the Lord. But we do have a mandate that is every bit as authoritative—it is an apostolic mandate that is also direct and imperative.

We, the church, have our mandate to proclaim the gospel to our fellow humans. May the Holy Spirit guide us that we may be obedient to our biblical obligation.

- We have lost our witness in modern society. Unfortunately, many within the church seem to have mislaid Romans 10. They seem mute when it comes to the gospel. During his closing days, the great English Particular Baptist preacher Charles Haddon Spurgeon lamented the state of the church as it drifted further from the gospel message:

> Everywhere there is apathy. Nobody cares whether that which is preached is true or false. A sermon is a sermon whatever the subject; only, the shorter the better.

Today, the modern problem for a person who delivers a sermon or teaches a Bible study class is not only time; it is also to avoid that very distressing of accusations—that of being boring. And to many people in churches, they see the gospel message as boring. Many think (erroneously) that they already know the gospel and do not need to hear it again. Others do not care if they know it or not—just don't expect them to share any of it with another human being.

Look, folks, let's just be honest with each other. Most of the people populating evangelical churches today do not exhibit the signs of being a true Christian. It seems as though their motivation for acquiring a perfect church experience is to: (1) assuage their guilty conscience; (2) be acceptable in their circle of friends, relatives, or acquaintances; and (3) keep from being bored. When they find a church that will give them all of that, they have found a church home—at least for a while, until that church violates one of the three points above. In the meantime, the gospel, which violates the "boring" part to these church-hoppers, many times goes unmentioned. The biblical mandate for the missionary work of the church is ignored. And the result is that the church becomes just like a country club or any other civic organization.

Is it any wonder that the church has very little, if any, influence within modern society? The church's power comes from its Maker and the One from whom its commission is given. But when the modern church consciously ignores God and His message for the ages, can it be a surprise that He should turn His back on the apostasy that is rampant in churches that claim to be Christian? We have lost our way, and because we refuse to follow the roadmap provided for us in the Scriptures, we have no way home.

- Salvation belongs to the Lord. Yet despite the apparent waywardness of the contemporary church, God will always have a remnant for Himself. Those He has purposefully intended to save before the foundation of the world will be saved. Those who were given to the Son for redemption will be brought home by the complete obedience and resurrection power of the Son. The gospel still stands. It cannot be altered by any humans to be twisted into a shape of their liking.

- We are in an impossible situation— unable not to sin. Yet our problem remains. Because of our nature since the fall of Adam and Eve, we are *non posse, non peccare.* Not able, not to sin. Because of our nature, we can, in and of ourselves, do nothing that pleases God and are "children of wrath" (Ephesians 2:1-3). Left to ourselves, we are doomed for condemnation and eternal torment in hell. And there is no sleight of hand or fancy moralistic principle that can change the situation. We cannot amuse and entertain ourselves out of our dire situation.

- We require a savior. We learn from God's word that we need a Savior. By ourselves we are hopeless. This is the "first half" of the gospel—the bad news. That we need help, a help that is beyond ourselves.

We need His mercy and His grace. And He sends it by way of His own Son, in the form of a man like us, so that He might be an acceptable sacrifice for our sins, that He might fully sympathize with our plight, and that He might impute His very righteousness, His holiness to our account. This is the gospel.

How we expect that we can replace this divine plan with one of our own making and still please God is the madness of a complete fool.

The Messiah has come! Let us welcome Him into our hearts so that we might find our way home.

Epilogue

The next day after the Friday night "Extreme" youth group meeting, one of the boys who had been in attendance, named Sam, was thinking about what had gone on the previous night, especially the words of the "senior youth pastor." *He said that God loves us and accepts us just the way we are.* Though not sure why, Sam was uneasy about that statement. Later he called his closest friend, Andy, who was also at the meeting, and posed the question to him. "It just doesn't sound right, Andy. I mean, if God accepts us just the way we are, what is church all about? Why do we even have a church if God is fine with us right now? What do you think?"

"Sam, you know you're the thinker. I mostly go to the meetings to see my friends and keep in touch. Since my dad took away my phone for a month, I can't text anyone, so school and the youth meetings are all I have left. Besides, we've had three different youth pastors in the last four years. I have a hard time keeping up with what any of them is talking about. The first one planned events and prayer vigils every weekend; the second was trying to make us all monks; and the one we have now is convinced that the way to 'grow the youth group' is through the music of the band."

"Well, I intend to do a little checking on this. It sounds really religious, but I don't know. Anyway, I'll see you at church tomorrow."

Later that afternoon Sam spoke with his father, who was a lay teacher and deacon at the church. He explained the situation and asked his father's opinion. "I think you've got a good question. You'll want to ask the youth pastor what he meant by what he said. Do him the courtesy of getting his personal explanation. But before that, if I were you, I'd do some checking myself so that you have a basis for your questions."

So Sam spent some time during the afternoon and evening reading parts of the Bible he had studied before, especially the gospel accounts and parts of the books of Romans and Ephesians. The next day he asked the senior youth pastor if they could meet, and when they did meet later that afternoon in his office at the church, Sam explained to him what his concerns were. The youth pastor stopped before answering and pulled his Bible off his shelf, spending several minutes going over the passage he used on Friday as well as others that Sam had mentioned. By the time their conference was over, the youth pastor had thanked Sam for his observations and his attention to the Scriptures. He promised to do some study and report back to Sam.

Three weeks later the two met again. The youth pastor admitted that Sam's discernment was right on target, and he planned to begin paying closer attention to what he was teaching. He asked Sam if he would consider being part of a team that helped prepare the lesson so that it would closely follow the Bible and adhere to solid Bible interpretation principles. Sam eagerly accepted and convinced some of his friends to join him.

Since that time the "Extreme" meetings on Friday nights took on a whole different atmosphere. The role of the music was reduced, and more time studying Scripture and spending time in prayer were added. The youth group lost some people, but gained many others, and the overall spiritual health was at an all-time high.

The following year the "Extreme" youth group, at their own instigation, disbanded completely and joined the various adult Bible study classes, becoming some of the most valuable contributors in each of the separate groups. The youth pastor became the new education minister for the church. He never failed to promote a right understanding of the Scriptures and a focus on the necessity of the gospel message and its full implications.

Cited Works

Piper, John. *God is the Gospel: Meditations on God's Love As the Gift of Himself.* Wheaton, Ill.: Crossway Books, 2005.

Sartelle, John. "Radically Contagious." *Tabletalk.* Vol.30, No.9. September, 2006.

Select Sermons of George Whitefield. "The Method of Grace." Carlisle, Pennsylvania: The Banner of Truth Trust, 1997.

I am astonished that you are so quickly deserting Him who called you in the grace of Christ and are turning to a different gospel—not that there is another one, but there are some who trouble you and want to distort the gospel of Christ. But even if we or an angel from heaven should preach to you a gospel contrary to the one we preached to you, let him be accursed. As we have said before, so now I say again: If anyone is preaching to you a gospel contrary to the one you received, let him be accursed.   (Galatians 1:6-9)

Also by Michael A. Thompson:

To Rome and Back With Martin Luther

and

*Outside the Camp: John Spilsbury, the
Pioneer of English Particular Baptists*
ISBN: 978-1456526-64-1

Charis Publications
P.O. Box 5116
Kingwood, TX 77325

www.ingramcontent.com/pod-product-compliance
Lightning Source LLC
Chambersburg PA
CBHW071817020426

42331CB00007B/1509